Colorado Aspens

Photography & Words by John Fielder

Westcliffe Publishers, Inc.
Englewood, Colorado

a Littlebook

First frontispiece: Scrub oak lend color to Winter's Aspen, Black Mesa

Second frontispiece: Autumn leaves rest along Middle Taylor Creek, Sangre de Cristo Range

Opposite: The morning moon rises over Brush Creek Valley, White River National Forest

Published by *Westcliffe Publishers, Inc.*
           2650 South Zuni Street
           Englewood, Colorado 80110
           Phone (303) 935-0900
Printed in   *Japan by Dai Nippon Printing Company, Ltd., Tokyo*
Copyright: *John Fielder, 1988*
International Standard Book Number:
ISBN 0-942394-81-X

If I ever lose my yearning to photograph the Colorado landscape, and I fervently hope the day never comes, I may eschew images of Spring wildflowers, I may tire of photographing cool mountain creeks, but I will never lose my infatuation with the Quaking Aspen tree. I may turn my back at the pale blue color of a morning sky, I may nap in the tent when an afternoon storm leaves the flora wet and chromatically succulent, but I will never resist the chance to photograph golden Aspen. That day will never come.

There is no scene with Aspen leaves, or Aspen groves, or great Aspen forests for which my camera will remain in the pack. I seem to always be able to find something colorful, something strangely symmetrical, something simply pleasing to the eye about the Aspen tree. It is a beautiful yet complicated plant. It has moods, but maintains a distinct personality from year to year. After almost eleven years of photographing the Aspen, one might think that I have seen every mood there is to see. Yet every new excursion to the mountain reveals new moods, and I don't think that nature's dynamic state is the only reason. I think I actually am perceiving things more acutely. The scene that I photographed five years ago might appear very different to me if I saw it today. Then I may have seen only the pale green budding leaves, but today I might also see subtle light reflecting from gray trunks.

The Aspen tree is so very dynamic. From Winter to Spring and Summer to Fall occur such profound visual changes that one might think it to be another tree. Though we hear most of its Autumn state, which is certainly a spectacular one, there is so much more to be enjoyed. Spring for the Aspen does not begin until late May or early June, depending upon elevation, when buds begin to open and lime green colored leaflets emerge. In two weeks the leaves grow to maturity. This transitory period is overlooked by most people, but for sheer visual magnificence it rivals Autumn. A perceptive eye will not only witness unusually translucent leaves brilliantly backlit by the sun, but also subtle shading of the forest in tones of green and gray as some trees leaf faster than others. As during Autumn, the days are cool and the water especially sweet from melting snows. It is a special time for many reasons, not the least important of which is one's inclination to look fervently forward to coming seasons.

Summer arrives quickly for the Quaking Aspen. By the middle of June, most leaves are reaching maturity and they will remain in this state for three months. The leaves assume a deep green color and lose much of their translucency as chlorophyll production increases. Yet Summer, too, is special as many things happen unique to that season. As usual the quaking leaves create the mood, though in summer I focus upon the singularly beautiful Aspen trunk. Heavy Summer showers soak its soft bark making its coloration rich and shiny as if varnished. It is then that one begins to perceive the different colors of bark from tree to tree and grove to grove. Brilliant whites give way to pale gray. Gray takes on tones of green in some forests. And in others, warm beiges pervade the forest. It may be an illusion, but all of the colors seem more lively in Summer, perhaps because the sap flows so freely.

By early September the air cools and the sun remains low in the sky, and several things begin to happen. For one, the days are shorter and chlorophyll production abates for lack of sufficient sunlight. The leaves can no longer remain green. Most turn yellow, though when exposed to extremely cold temperatures some turn brown. Some leaves even turn red. The entire process takes up to four weeks and from one week to the next a grove inherits a new mood, a new visual character. Perhaps the most exciting thing for me is to see the juxtaposition of one color next to another. Within one single grove, one may see greens of summer, yellows and orange, browns, and variations of each of these in between. As if painted with a brush, patterns of color are formed with subtle shading easing the transition from one color to the next. The result can be nothing less than a natural work of art.

The colors of Autumn manifest themselves best on cloudy days. No less spectacular are the brilliant colors created when direct sunlight shines through the leaves. Called backlighting, the effect is unparalleled in nature. Those translucent leaves assume visual properties that must be seen to be believed, properties that even the most proficient of photographers struggles to preserve on film.

Brisk winds of late Autumn blow most of the leaves from the Aspen by the second week in October. Stripped of what makes most of their personality, one might now stay home and leave the tree until Spring arrives. But this would certainly be a mistake in judgement. Great things are about to happen to the Aspen and there are no less than six months to enjoy them. Bereft of leaves, one can now clearly focus upon the shape of the core of this tree. The sight of hundreds of parallel trunks, tall and thin, rising straight to the sky with little deviation, can be overwhelming. These barren trunks in mass form one of nature's greatest patterns, one of its most intense studies of shape and form, and with almost complete disregard to chromatic consideration. And what a sight it is when moist air covers these stark inhabitants of a Winter world with transparent ice.

Perhaps the greatest joys to be derived from the Quaking Aspen tree lie beyond visual and botanical conditions. I retain prodigious memories of glorious Spring foliage and overwhelming Autumn colors; yet memories of my own mood, recollection of how my senses of smell and taste worked while making breakfast in the forest seem to pervade the visual remains. I surmise from this fact that the visual aspects of the landscape and its floral denizens are important to me, for in them I am allowed to be creative with my camera, but that the real joy is derived more from the moment of just being there. The smell of the leaves, the aural aspects of rustling leaves, the sight of them moving, the coolness of the wind on my face, the taste of the food in my mouth, the peace found in falling asleep in a grove of Aspen, they make the best memories.

John Fielder

Though dormant I am now in cold
My leaves they took a grasp to hold
In wind, in snow, through all I know
Just nothing seems to make them go

White River National Forest

'Tis winter and it's much too long
To pass the time without a song
But since we have no wind to play
I think we'll sketch ourselves today

near Steamboat Springs

Overleaf: *Aspen protect a cold ridge above Telluride*

A mess we are of dried up limbs
I think that if I had a whim
I'd hope for leaves to grow on me
So it's remembered I'm a tree

near Trapper's Lake

It won't be long 'till Spring will come
So take a glance before the sun
Revives the juice to make young buds
Release their leaves and thoughts of love

❧

on Grand Mesa

4

'Twas only one short month ago
When snow put on the only show
But now my limbs are back in shape
And what a show they've learned to make

above Telluride

It's clear I am so delicate
Because of water oh so wet
You wonder why we are so green
It's water in the closeby stream

White River National Forest

By now you must have known my life
Is free from common pain and strife
For life below these snowcapped peaks
Brings peace of mind from week to week

San Juan Mountains

That fence will fail to keep me in
For underground my roots do swim
To nothing there will they soon yield
Before I'm in the other field

below Wolf Creek Pass

A tree of thirst I am for sure
I drink of rain that falls so pure
Summer is dry I do depend
On water lest I meet my end

along Cucharas Pass

Where water flows I take my place
I spread thin roots no time to waste
Though soon no water will remain
For me to spread my great domain

below Lizard Head Peak

In Spring the sheep return to graze
On grass so thick it takes them days
The cabin is released from snow
A place for herdsmen now to go

Sneffels Range

Overleaf: *Nature paints patterns in the forest, Grand Mesa*

Through groves of green the road proceeds
Beneath great trees with summer leaves
They quake so gently in the wind
I hope this road will never end

Sangre de Christo Range

The trunks they have great character
So straight and tall I do prefer
And summer rain is finally back
To coat the trunks as if shellac

Sawatch Range

Though straight and tall I do prefer
I like the ones that aren't so sure
So thin and frail they tend to go
In directions fast winds blow

Gunnison National Forest

Close looks reveal a face beset
With marks I soon will not forget
The source of which I'm not aware
And try to guess I do not dare

along the Crystal River

A sun that's low within the sky
Is nature's biggest reason why
My leaves begin to turn to gold
For all the world to now behold

along the West Dolores River

So slowly does the change begin
For rushing now would be a sin
The glory of what is to come
Will pique the sense of everyone

Sneffels Range

My changing leaves are not alone
In ways to show you countless tones
For here you see a Fall sunset
With color you'll not soon forget

San Juan Mountains

My leaves remain alone quite high
They try to touch the clear blue sky
For here the rays will bring me life
To see the sun is my great strife

San Miguel Mountains

Great winds they rob me of my leaves
Needless to say I am bereaved
But when they fell to make this view
I felt I'd lost so very few

above Telluride

Still water makes me thirsty still
I'm tempted now to take my fill
But if I drink it will be gone
Reflections of my Autumn song

below Sierra Blanca Peak

Overleaf: *The thickest*
of groves prepares for winter, Sangre de Cristo Range

No gem I know can try to vie
With blue from in the Autumn sky
My golden leaves they look so fine
When Autumn blue appears behind

along Kebler Pass

I will remind you once again
That color's not my only end
For when the leaves are on the ground
I still can make your head spin round

Grand Mesa

The snows will soon return for long
But now I play my Autumn song
As flakes do rest along my boughs
I wait for winter to arouse

White River National Forest

My leaves resist the change to come
They want to stay 'till winter's done
But soon new leaves will see the sun
The cycle then will start to run

White River National Forest